Take a trip to
GREECE

Keith Lye
General Editor
Henry Pluckrose

Franklin Watts
London   New York   Sydney   Toronto

Words about Greece

Acropolis
Aegean Sea
Apollo

bouzoukia

Corfu
Corinth Canal
Cyclades
   Islands

Delphi
Dodecanese
   Islands
drachma

Eastern
   Orthodox
   Church

Ionian Islands

Kárpathos

lepta

mandolin
Meteora
Míkonos
monastery
monk

Naxos

Omonia Square
oracle

Panathenaic
   stadium

Parthenon
Pindus
   Mountains
pinnacles
Piraeus
priests

Rhodes
ruins

Santorini

tavernas
Thessaly
Thíra

Zeus

Franklin Watts Limited
12a Golden Square
London W1R 4BA

ISBN UK Edition: 0 85166 983 2
ISBN US Edition: 531–03759–2
Library of Congress Catalog
Card No: 83-60903

© Franklin Watts Limited 1982
Reprinted 1983

Typeset by Ace Filmsetting Ltd.,
Frome, Somerset
Printed in Great Britain by
E. T. Heron, Essex and London

Maps: Tony Payne
Design and Editorial Services:
Grub Street
Photographs: Zefa; D. Turner, 10;
J. Allan Cash, 19; Coloursport, 24.

Athens, the modern Greek capital, was the chief city in ancient Greece, a great early civilization. Ancient Athens was at the height of its power about 2,430 years ago. Many ruins survive, like the Parthenon, a temple on a hill called the Acropolis.

Modern buildings overlook Omonia Square in the heart of Athens. Athens is by far the largest city in Greece. Greater Athens, has a population of 2.5 million. Many tourists visit Athens.

Piraeus is the leading port of Greece. It lies within Greater Athens. Piraeus exports many products including olive oil and wine. Ships leave from Piraeus for the many Greek islands. Piraeus is also an important industrial area.

Much of Greece is mountainous. The highest peak is Mount Olympus, in northern Greece. It is 2,917 m. (9,570 feet) above sea level. In ancient times, the Greeks believed that gods lived on the top.

These rocky pinnacles are at Meteora in the province of Thessaly. The Pindus Mountains, which form the backbone of northern Greece, can be seen in the distance. The plains of Thessaly are very fertile.

This picture shows some stamps and money used in Greece. The main unit of currency is the drachma, which is divided into 100 lepta.

Corfu (Kérkira in Greek) is one of the beautiful Greek Ionian Islands situated off the west coast. Corfu has many fine beaches which attract tourists especially during the hot, dry summers. About 5 million tourists visit Greece every year.

Tourists sit at a seaside restaurant on the island of Míkonos. Míkonos is in the Cyclades Islands in the Aegean Sea, which lies to the east of the Greek mainland. Islands are about one-fifth the area of Greece.

One-third of Greece is cultivated and two out of every five people work on farms. The chief crops are citrus fruits (including oranges), grapes, olives, tobacco and wheat. Greece is one of Western Europe's poorer countries.

A goatherd leads his flock to pasture on the rocky island of Thíra (or Santorini). Greece has about four million goats, eight million sheep and one million cattle. Most goats and sheep are kept in the upland areas.

The notices in this butcher's shop are in Greek. The Greek alphabet has 24 letters. The Roman alphabet, in which this book is printed, has 26.

The Greeks have been a seafaring people since ancient times. These fishermen live on Kárpathos in the Dodecanese Islands, off the west coast of Turkey. Fishing is a major industry. Apart from fish, sponges are also gathered from the sea.

Many kinds of fresh vegetables are on sale at this open-air market in the town of Corfu. Fruit is plentiful throughout Greece.

Villagers follow traditional crafts and their work is sold in the towns. It includes hand-made clothes, pottery and tiles, lace, embroidery and necklaces. Workers pass on their skills to their children.

17

This family runs a village guest house for tourists on Crete, the largest Greek island. Crete has many places to visit, including seaside resorts and the ruins of palaces that date back more than 3,400 years.

Greek children start school at the age of six. The government provides primary school education for children between the ages of 6–12. Secondary education ends at the age of 18.

Tourists sit at the next table to some local people in a bar on Míkonos. Even in the hottest weather, most elderly Greeks wear formal clothes when they go out. Greek women often wear black dresses and cover their heads with scarves.

Donkeys and motor scooters are popular means of transport in Greece. This donkey is carrying a skin bag filled with wine. This picture was taken on Naxos, the largest island in the Cyclades group.

Many houses in Greece, as here at the port of Piraeus, are white-washed to protect them from the sun. About three out of every five people in Greece live in cities and towns.

Restaurants called tavernas are popular meeting places for tourists and local people alike. The country's warm climate allows people to eat in the open air for most of the year. But most people prefer to sit in the shade on hot, summer days.

Soccer is the most popular sport in Greece. The largest grounds are in Athens and Piraeus. League matches are played on Sunday afternoons. Many who do not go to the matches follow them on radio or television.

These Greek dancers are wearing national dress. Dancing is a pastime enjoyed by many people. The music is often provided by the bouzoukia, an instrument similar to a mandolin.

This is a large Greek oil tanker. Greece has one of the world's largest merchant fleets, with about 4,000 vessels. They earn a lot of money for the country. Ship-building is a major industry. Manufactured goods are the most valuable exports.

The Corinth Canal links the Gulf of Corinth to the Saronic Gulf. It shortens the journey from the Adriatic Sea to Piraeus.

A view of Athens shows the columns of the temple of the god Zeus. Nearby is the Panathenaic stadium, where the 1896 Olympic Games were held.

The ruins of this temple of the god Apollo are at Delphi, a religious city in ancient Greece. People came here to learn about the future. A woman oracle made strange sounds. These were said to be the words of Apollo. Priests explained what they meant.

This Christian Eastern Orthodox Church is on Rhodes in the Dodecanese Islands. Most Greeks belong to the Eastern Orthodox Church.

Monasteries were built hundreds of years ago on rock pinnacles at Meteora in Thessaly. Each monastery had cells for the monks and one or two churches. Food was hauled up by rope. Four monasteries are still used.

Index

Aegean Sea 11
Alphabet, Greek 14
Apollo 29
Athens 3–5, 28

Bouzoukia 25

Church 30
Corfu 10, 16
Corinth Canal 27
Crete 18
Cyclades Islands 11, 21

Dancing 25
Delphi 29
Dodecanese Islands 15, 30
Donkeys 21

Exports 5, 26

Farming 12–13
Fishing 15

Goats 13
Greek gods 6, 29

Houses 22

Industry 5, 26
Ionian Islands 10, 16

Kárpathos 15

Meteora 7, 31
Míkonos 11, 20
Monasteries 31
Money 8

Naxos 21

Oil tanker 26
Olympic Games 28
Olympus, Mount 6

Parthenon 3
Pindus Mountains 7
Piraeus 5, 22, 27

Religion 29–31
Rhodes 30

Schools 19
Shipping 5, 26–27
Soccer 24
Stamps 8

Thessaly 7, 31
Thíra 13
Tourism 4, 10–11, 18, 20, 23, 31

JUL 0 5 1985

J949.5076

9 IDA WILLIAMS

Lye, Keith.
    Take a trip to Greece / Keith Lye ;
general editor, Henry Pluckrose. --
London ; New York : F. Watts, c1982.
    32 p. : col. ill. ; 22 cm.
    Includes index.
    Summary: Text and photographs present
aspects of Greece's geography,
industries, education, and sights of
tourist interest.
    ISBN 0-531-03759-2 (U.S.)

    1. Greece--Description and travel--
1981-   --Juvenile literature.
I. Pluckrose, Henry Arthur. II. Title

R00178 45267

GA   15 MAY 85   9996957 GAPApc   83-60903